W9-BMH-840

WE LAUGH, WE LOVE, WE CRY

CHILDREN LIVING WITH MENTAL RETARDATION

FRANKLIN PIERCE
COLLEGE LIBRARY
RINDGE, N.H. 03461

DON'T
TURN
AWAY

For a free color catalog describing Gareth Stevens' list of high-quality children's books call 1-800-433-0942.

Library of Congress Cataloging-in-Publication Data

Bergman, Thomas, 1947-
   We laugh, we love, we cry.

   (Don't turn away)
   Translation of: Vem fôrstár oss.
   Summary: Describes the home life, physiotherapy, and schooling of two mentally retarded sisters.
   1. Mentally handicapped children--Juvenile literature. [1. Mentally handicapped]
I. Title. II. Series: Bergman, Thomas, 1947-   . Don't turn away.
HQ773.7.B4713   1988   362.3'088054   88-42971
ISBN 1-55532-914-4

CURR
HQ
773.7
.B4713
1989

◇ D O N 'T
T U R N
A W Ā Y ◇

North American edition first published in 1989 by

Gareth Stevens, Inc.
7317 West Green Tree Road
Milwaukee, Wisconsin 53223, USA

First published in Swedish in 1977 by LiberFörlag under the title *Vem fôrstár oss*.

Copyright © 1989 this format, by Gareth Stevens, Inc.
Photographs and original text copyright © 1977 by Thomas Bergman
Additional text and design copyright © 1989 by Gareth Stevens, Inc.

All rights reserved. No part of this book may be reproduced in any form or by any means without permission in writing from Gareth Stevens, Inc.

Series Editor: MaryLee Knowlton
Research Editor: Scott Enk
Series Designer: Kate Kriege

Printed in the United States of America

1 2 3 4 5 6 7 8 9 95 94 93 92 91 90 89

WE LAUGH, WE LOVE, WE CRY

CHILDREN LIVING WITH MENTAL RETARDATION

DON'T
TURN
AWAY

Thomas Bergman

Gareth Stevens Children's Books
MILWAUKEE

When Thomas Bergman first showed me the remarkable photographs that appear in We Laugh, We Love, We Cry, I was struck by their power to capture the essence of children's personalities and moods. As we looked at them together — I for the first time, he once again after many times — I was moved by the intensity and passion of a person who cares deeply about children who are mentally retarded.

Thomas is Sweden's best-known children's photographer, with a reputation stretching from Europe to Japan. His compassion, admiration, and affection for children with disabilities inspired him to embark on a special photographic mission. The striking black-and-white photographs you will see in this book will remain in your memory. The thoughts and feelings that Thomas' young friends have shared with him form the basis for the insightful text that accompanies the pictures.

You will meet children in the pages of this book with a disability that may be unfamiliar to you. You will be inspired by the originality and courage with which they meet the challenges presented by this disability. And you will be moved by the many ways that they are like children everywhere. I hope you will ask yourself, as I did, "Why haven't I met many children like these? Where are they? Why don't I see them in the schools and on playgrounds, in museums and shopping malls, on the streets and in the parks?" These are the questions we must explore. Our communities should embrace all people. We will _all_ be the richer for it.

In We Laugh, We Love, We Cry, Asa and Anna Karin show us that a disability should not be a cause for embarrassment, separation, and fear. Instead, it should be a reason for reaching out, sharing the joys, sorrows, and hopes of our lives.

Gareth Stevens
PUBLISHER

ASA

This is Asa, five years old. Asa is mentally retarded. She has trouble understanding the world as most people understand it and is slow to learn. In addition, she has physical problems that have made moving about difficult for her. And she cannot talk.

During the first year of her life, Asa hardly moved at all. When she was a year old her parents took her to a clinic for children who are born with disabilities. The therapist there looked carefully at Asa, and said what her parents had hoped to hear: "Asa will learn to walk."

For the next three years, Asa and her therapist, Sabina, worked together. The therapy was difficult — tiring and sometimes painful. By the time she was 18 months old, Asa could roll over and hold things in her hands. At two, she could sit alone and stand if Sabina held her hands. When she was three, Asa could walk holding onto a doll's carriage. At four she took her first stumbling steps all by herself.

ANNA KARIN

Asa's six-year-old sister, Anna Karin, has the same disabilities that Asa has. She began physical therapy when she was seven months old and was two before she could walk by herself. She cannot talk, either, but she is learning to communicate with sign language.

Asa and Anna Karin have had many teachers and therapists already. These people have told their parents that the girls' receptive language is much greater than their expressive language. This means that they can understand much more of what goes on around them than they can tell you about. Sometimes people don't realize how much the girls can understand.

This book is about Asa and Anna Karin. Through pictures of them and the people in their lives, we can try to understand what they cannot tell us in words.

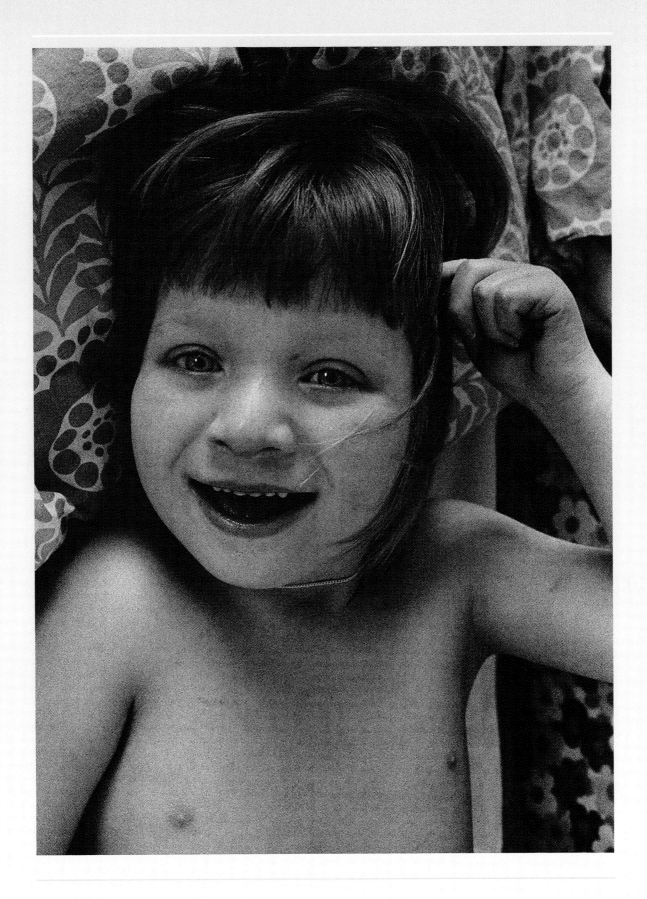

On weekend mornings, everyone sleeps in until the girls decide it's time to get up. Then they crawl into bed with their parents to cuddle and talk about what to do on this sunny day. Asa and Anna Karin's mother and father are getting to be good at communicating with their daughters. They talk, use signs, and watch for the girls' reactions to see what they're trying to tell them. The family decides to go to the museum today.

This family is warm and close because they love each other. They depend very much on each other to understand what each person needs.

Because the girls look unusual and walk differently, the whole family does not see as many other people as they would like. They are all sensitive about being stared at or avoided. They prefer that people come up to them and ask questions if they have them instead of staring or turning away. Then they can talk, and no one will feel so uncomfortable.

Since Anna Karin began learning sign language, the world has opened up for her. Here she tells her father that she wants a red crayon. Before learning sign language, she had to point and wait until he could figure out what she meant. Having no way to express yourself is frustrating. Now her vocabulary is growing with her ability to understand and her parents feel they are getting to know her in a whole new way. They can tell much more about what she is thinking. This encourages her to think even more.

Physical therapy has been part of Anna Karin's life since she was a tiny baby. Twice a week, she goes by taxi to a clinic. She likes the trip and waves happily to her mother standing at the window. Anna Karin is quite comfortable traveling by herself and meeting the therapists, doctors, and teachers. This is how her life has always been.

Today Anna Karin's therapist, Lena, is taping Anna Karin's feet for the first time. Asa's therapist, Kerstin, shows them how she does Asa's feet. Anna Karin will have to keep the tape on until bedtime. The tape will help her feet move in the right direction, much the way braces help teeth move slowly into place. Anna Karin is a little anxious about the new procedure and is glad when Lena hugs her and says it's over.

Lena tries to make therapy as much like playing as she can. But therapy is not play. It is hard, important work. At first, Anna Karin's body did not want to walk or stretch or push. She has had to teach it to do these things, and it has been a struggle. And the struggle will continue as she learns to run, jump, and do all the things normal bodies seem to just grow into.

Asa, too, goes to therapy twice a week. She waits eagerly at the window until she sees the taxi. Her driver is Harriet, someone she recognizes, so going alone is no problem for her. Asa learns from routines and depends upon them for security. When her mother tells her it is Tuesday or Friday, she knows she is going to therapy. When routines change, Asa becomes confused and frightened.

Much of Asa's therapy takes place in front of a mirror so she can see what she is doing. Her favorite part of the routine is trying on hats. She tries to make this part last a long time because it's so much fun.

Asa keeps her mouth open too much, so she always wears a bib because she is so slobbery.

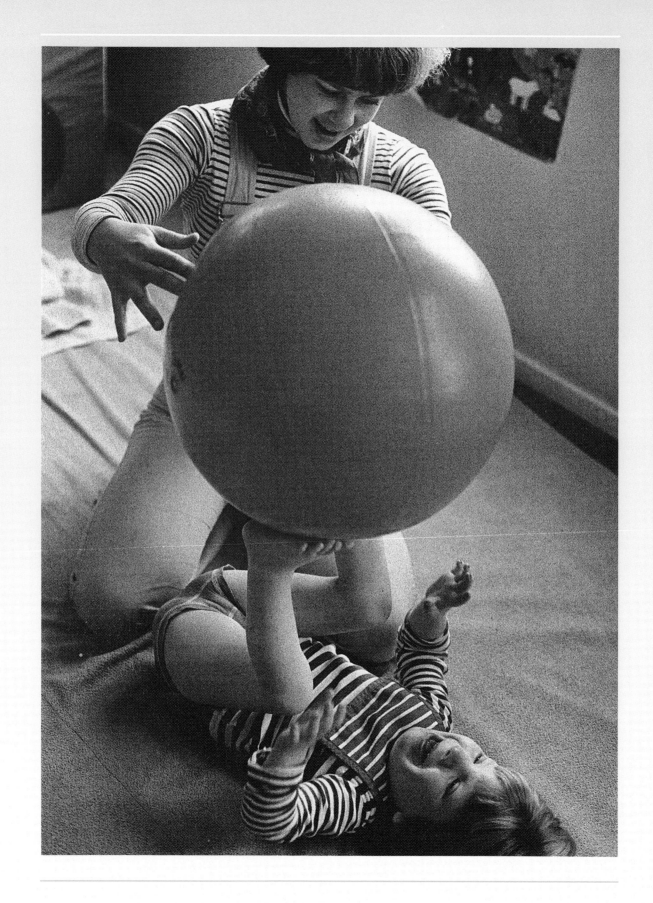

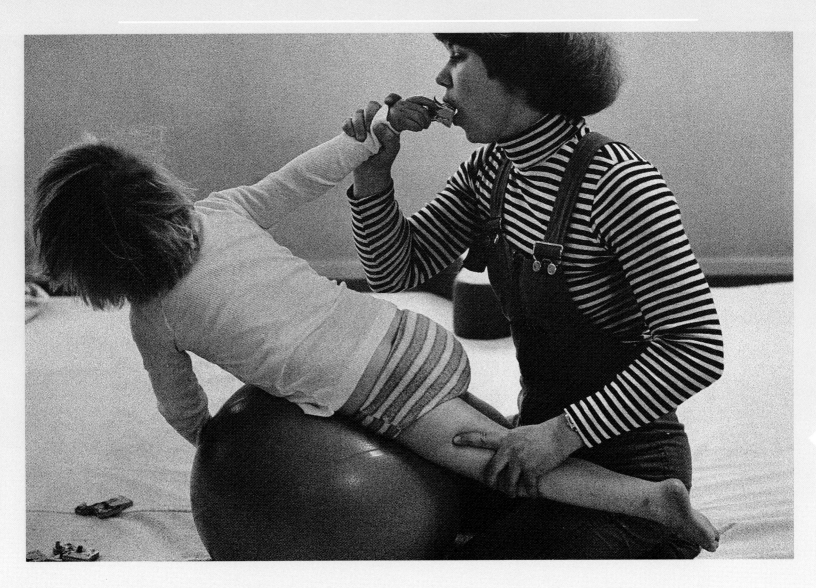

Asa's therapy involves working with a big ball. When she and Kerstin start the therapy, it's like playing. But soon it's hard work. Asa is always very tired after therapy.

Today's routine is helping Asa develop her reaching and balancing skills. Kerstin supports her on the ball as Asa leans in one direction and twists her arm back to get a toy. This will strengthen her torso and neck muscles. You might think Asa would be afraid of falling, but she and Kerstin have worked together a long time. Asa trusts her therapist.

Asa's feet are taped at the end of her therapy session. She's an old hand
at this and enjoys the foot massage that comes with the taping. The taping
helps her to put her whole foot down when she walks so she doesn't walk
only on her tiptoes. She finds having her feet taped very exciting. She
watches carefully to be sure it's done the way she expects. This is
something she knows.

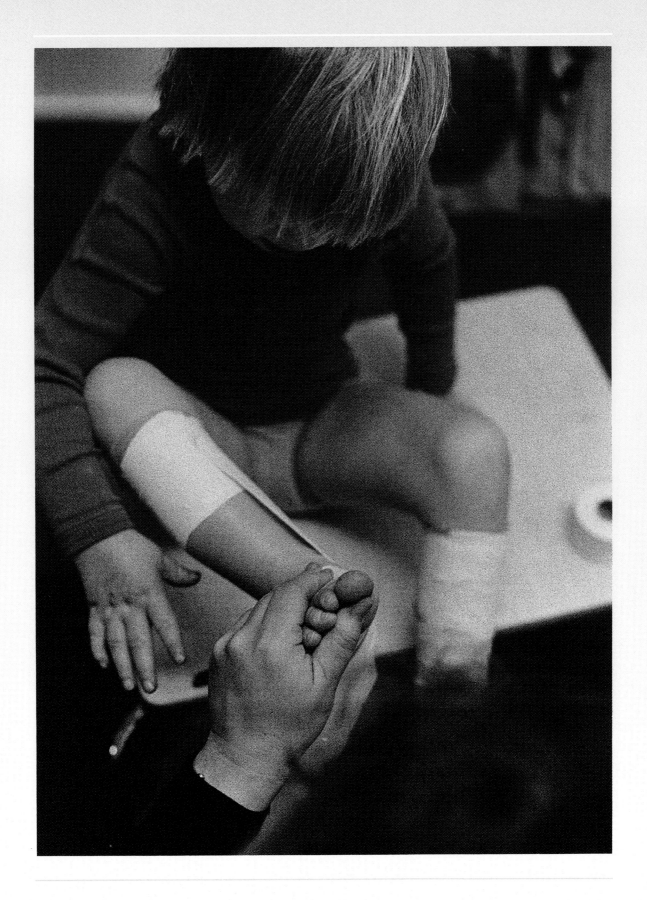

The relationship between a child and a physical therapist is special. Often Kerstin has to push and prod Asa into doing things that wear her out and even hurt her. Some sessions have ended with Asa sobbing with frustration and fatigue. There will probably be more like these. But without the therapy, Asa would not have walked.

Asa is happy when her therapy is over. Even though she and Kerstin have had a good session, it is tiring. They both demand a lot from each other, and sometimes the sessions do not go smoothly. But they understand each other and like each other. This is important because Asa will need Kerstin for a long time.

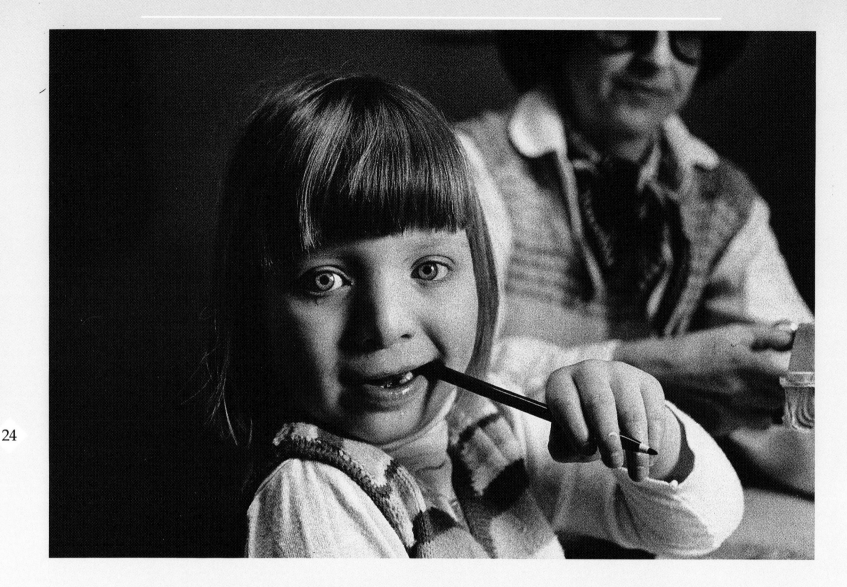

From the time Anna Karin was very young, she attended a school for
retarded children. She was in what is called an early intervention program.
This means that people intervene, or work with the children, early in their
lives to help them make the most of their abilities. Educating children
early, when their difficulties become known, gives them a head start. It
trains their minds and bodies to try harder than they might if they were
left alone until they were of school age and had well-developed habits.

Now Anna Karin goes to an ordinary kindergarten and gets her therapies at a clinic. She could have them at school, but she needs many kinds. So her parents prefer that she stay in her classroom and not spend so much of the school day in therapy.

Many children with disabilities must learn to be more independent than other children their age. They take cabs or special buses to therapists and teachers before they are old enough for kindergarten. They learn to get along with many types of professionals while they are still very young.

On Anna Karin's first day of kindergarten, her mother was sick and couldn't take her. Anna Karin insisted on going and signed that she would go alone. So she did, on her own school bus. And everything was fine.

Anna Karin often watches the other children play. They can talk to each other and run, but Anna Karin cannot. So she can't join in all their games. But in things like painting, jigsaw puzzles, playing house, and listening to stories and music, she does as well as the other children do.

Sometimes Anna Karin's teacher, Ingrid, invites her home after school to play with her children. This is special for both families. For Anna Karin, it is important because it is nice to have some place besides home where she is understood. Ingrid understands sign language, and Anna Karin is helping her teach it to her children so everybody can communicate.

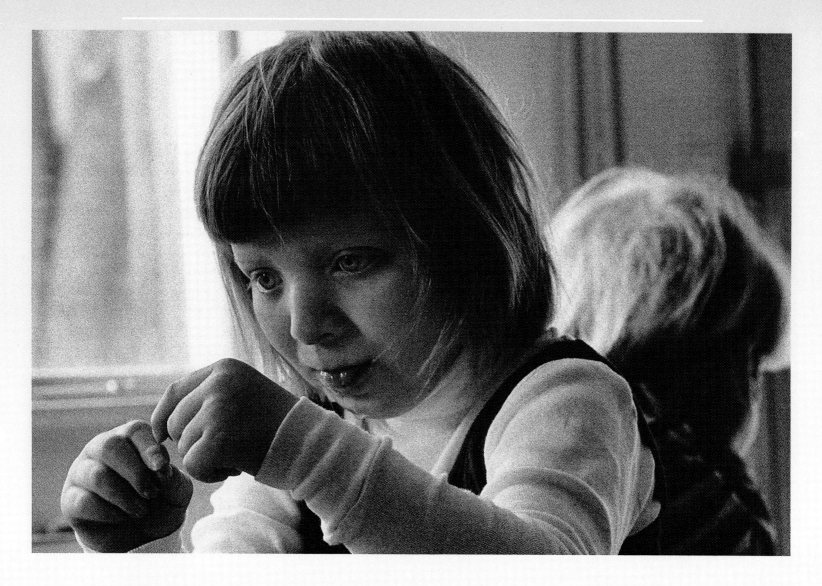

Anna Karin misses having a friend. Other children her age are free to pick their friends and to decide when to play with them and when to play alone. Anna Karin would like this to be part of her life too, but it is not. None of the children in her class know sign language, so they don't seem to think of her as someone to invite over to play with after school.

Anna Karin's mother sometimes invites children from the class over and that works out for a while. But even there Anna Karin feels left out and jealous of the others who can talk and can play more complicated games.

People often don't realize how much Anna Karin understands. One day a mother driving some of the children home after school invited them in for juice and cookies. She didn't include Anna Karin, so she drove her home first. Anna Karin knew what was happening. She was hurt and disappointed. When they reached her house, she cried and refused to get out of the car. Her mother came to meet her at the car. As she realized what was happening, tears came to her eyes, too.

Anna Karin and her mother have an appointment today with a doctor and a speech therapist to evaluate her speech abilities. Anna Karin is a little shy. She is also worried that something may hurt, so she needs a little time to relax. The doctor and therapist let her explore the room by herself, listening to her and watching her signing.

Then Britta, the therapist, shows Anna Karin pictures on cards and asks her what she can see. Anna Karin replies with signs. The therapist is encouraged that Anna Karin recognizes so many of the pictures.

The doctor examines Anna Karin's mouth and throat to see if anything about their structure is keeping her from talking. He says everything looks fine.

The doctor and therapist both feel it is important to train Anna Karin to make speech sounds as well as to sign. When the appointment is over, Anna Karin's mother asks how well she will be able to talk. The doctor says he doesn't know.

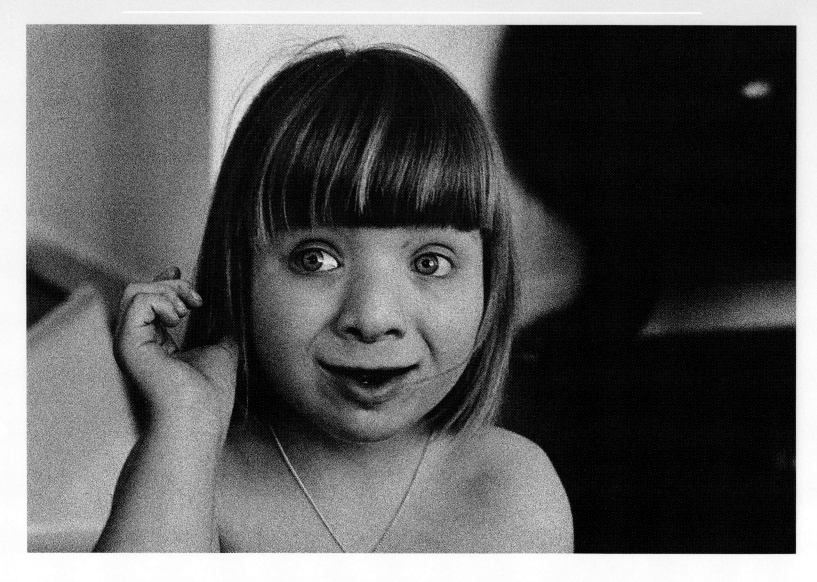

Twice a week, Anna Karin has training in using sign language. Her teacher comes to the school to meet with her. In the six months that she has been studying sign language, Anna Karin has learned over 200 signs, some for words and some for phrases and concepts, or ideas. Her parents are studying, too, trying to keep ahead of her.

Anna Karin can understand most of what her parents and the children in her class talk about. Before she knew how to sign she was often angry or sad, because she could not make people understand her. But now she is usually able to make people understand what hurts, what she wants to eat, when she is feeling sick, what she did in school, and what she will be doing on the weekend.

Asa spends her days at a day-care center. Her classmates are not mentally retarded. She has learned to dress herself and serve herself at the table. She usually helps set the table, too, and brings the food back into the kitchen. She is beginning to learn signs. Her classmates and teachers are learning, too. The way they are learning is informal. Asa learns from her parents and then teaches her teachers and friends. Each day they sit in a circle and learn a few new signs.

Having friends is as important to Asa as it is to anyone else. When no one plays with her, she sits on the floor by herself. Asa likes it when the other children play with her. Sometimes they play house and let her be the baby. Other times the older girls play hairdresser and fix her hair.

Sometimes the children's games are confusing for Asa. It takes her longer than it takes the others to learn them. Sometimes, just as she finally figures out how a game is played, the others lose interest and move on to something else. But even though she gets frustrated, her parents think it's better for her to adjust to the pace of the normal world instead of living in a slower one of her own.

It's time for lunch. Asa had been hungry, but the teacher said they could go sledding after lunch. So now Asa is so excited she can't eat a thing. She gets up from the table immediately and heads for the door. Her teacher calls to her but Asa's mind is made up.

After lunch the children brush their teeth and wash up. Asa is learning how to take care of herself. Learning these living skills will help her be independent and more like other children. It's important to fit in. But Asa does it her way: wearing a firefighter's hat, she brushes her teeth with great vigor. She pretends they are burning and she's putting out the fire with her toothbrush.

Asa loves sledding. But walking in the snow is exhausting for her. She needs a hand to hold onto to climb back up the hill. When she falls in the snow, and she falls often, she has a lot of trouble getting back up. Sometimes her friends try to help her up and everybody falls in a heap.

Back in the classroom, cold and wet clothes come off and everyone relaxes, tired and happy.

The day is done. Two sisters return home from busy days. They're glad to see each other — most of the time. The two don't always get along perfectly. They can't argue or yell at each other, though, so when they're angry, they pinch.

The days are full and busy for Asa and Anna Karin. They have to work harder than most of us to get where they're going. Sometimes they don't seem to be going very fast, but they are going steadily. As the girls learn to express themselves and the people around them learn to understand them, the rewards of their work will come to them.

QUESTIONS FROM CHILDREN ABOUT MENTAL RETARDATION

Here are some answers to questions children have asked about mental retardation and how it affects people. Maybe you've wondered about some of these things, too.

What is mental retardation?

Perhaps you have been told that mentally retarded people are "slow learners." This is true, but it means more than that, too. People who are mentally retarded will be slow to develop physical skills as well as mental skills. Also, they will develop some mental skills more easily than others.

Often mental retardation is measured by how well a person performs on a test. We usually call these IQ tests because they are designed to measure the intelligence quotient, or the ability to understand. Average intelligence has a quotient, or number, of 100. Mental retardation begins somewhere below 90. The quotient for labeling a person mentally retarded can vary between 75 and 90, depending on who wants to know. Different government agencies and education systems use different numbers to label a person.

There are different degrees of mental retardation. Mildly retarded people can learn to read and write. They can also learn the skills they need to hold a job, take care of themselves, and raise children.

More severely retarded people may require constant care in an institution for their whole lives. Usually these people have serious physical disabilities as well as below-normal intelligence. Not all of the people confined in institutions today need this kind of care. They and people who care about them are working hard to get them out of the institutions and back into their communities.

How does an IQ test work?

There are many kinds of IQ tests to evaluate people at different ages and with different backgrounds. Experts in child development have decided what children should be able to understand by the time they reach a certain age. Let's say a little boy is four. The experts say he should be able to understand certain concrete concepts or basic ideas. For example, he should be able to look at a picture of a tractor and say that it is, indeed, a tractor. He should not say it is a cow or a peanut.

He should also be able to understand some abstract concepts, difficult ideas. For example, he should be able to look at a picture of a man in a firefighter's hat and say that his job is to put out fires. The concept is abstract because the child must think about something he cannot see, the fires, rather than just identify what he sees.

Very young children think in concrete terms. This means they know what they see. The ability to think abstractly develops as they grow older. A mentally retarded person's ability for abstract thinking does not usually develop as well as that of a person with normal intelligence.

IQ tests measure people's ability to think in these two ways according to how well they are expected to think at their age. Young children are given tests with pictures and toys. The person giving the test asks questions or gives directions and takes note of the child's responses. A good test will show what a child understands and can respond to correctly.

Are there any problems with IQ tests?

A test that asks too many questions about things that are not part of a child's experience will not measure abilities accurately. For example, a four-year-old girl who is asked about a picture of a woman in an apron might not be able to answer it if her mother has never worn an apron.

Most good tests include enough questions that one or two questions like this will not affect the child's score. But in the past, tests were best suited to children who grew up in white English-speaking families with two parents. Children with different backgrounds got lower scores. Sometimes this still happens today. There are tests for children with all kinds of backgrounds, but people have to know enough about the child to pick the right one.

Other things can affect a person's score on a test. Children who do not hear well may not have learned as much by the age of four as children with normal hearing. But their ability to learn may be greater than the test score shows. Children with speaking problems may not be able to say all that they understand. Their scores also will not be accurate measures of their abilities.

Many testers believe that they must use more than one test and test a child at different times and in different settings to get a really good measure of what this child can do.

What causes mental retardation?
Most people who are mentally retarded have been that way since birth. Something in the way they developed while inside their mothers determined their condition.

It may be an inherited condition — that is, contained in the genes that came together from the mother and father at conception. Or it may be a result of illness or injury to the mother while she was pregnant. Children whose mothers abused alcohol or cocaine while they were pregnant are very likely to be mentally retarded and to have other problems.

Brain injury from beatings or accidents can also result in permanent mental retardation. The cause of most mental retardation is unknown.

Do children who are mentally retarded know it?
Most children who are mentally retarded know something about it. They see their friends and younger brothers and sisters learning things easily while the rules of games and social skills come harder to them. Their parents and teachers may have discussed their disability with them. Sadly, they may know because other people have called them names and made fun of them.

Despite knowing they are different, most children who are retarded want very much to play with other children. To include them you might have to explain things more carefully or make the activity simple or find a special role for this special child.

One thing you should know: Mentally retarded children who are not allowed to play with you or who are laughed at or treated cruelly know what is happening. They may keep coming around looking for another chance. This doesn't mean they are not being hurt. They just want so badly to be one of the group that they'll risk being hurt again.

Are retarded people more gentle and loving than other people?
Not really. They may seem more trusting and more accepting of what happens to them. But everybody's personality is different. Gentle, loving people are generally people who have been raised and treated with love.

What can I talk about or do with a person who is mentally retarded?
Do what you would if you met another person your age — see what you have in common. Do you both like music? Baseball cards? Collect anything? Wear make-up? Work in the garden? Eat pizza? Ride bikes? Go to movies? These are all things a mentally retarded child can participate in, often as well as you do — and as happily.

What is the difference between mental retardation and mental illness?

People with mental illness do not always see what is happening clearly. Problems with their thinking and feelings keep them from knowing what is real and what is only in their head. Mental illness can come and go and can often be controlled with medicine and counseling. Sometimes it cannot.

Mental illness has nothing to do with intelligence. Anybody can become mentally ill. Mentally retarded people learn more slowly than others, but they see the world as it really is. Mentally ill people have times when they do not.

Are people with mental retardation able to use or learn from computers?

Yes. Often a computer is a terrific teacher! You may have already discovered this yourself.

Because they learn more slowly, mentally retarded children need to have things repeated many times and need to take many tries to learn. A computer does not become impatient. Some programs can vary the approach if the child cannot learn one way. Good computer programs, with their bright colors, designs, and funny noises, hold children's attention and keep them from losing interest until they learn the lesson.

Computers are also great for people who can't speak clearly. Some retarded children can understand much more than they can tell about. Some have trouble talking but can use a computer to express ideas that would otherwise remain bottled up in their heads.

Isn't it better for mentally retarded people to be with others like them so they can have good care?

Most retarded people, including many still confined in institutions, do not benefit from being denied the right to make their own choices about their lives. Mental retardation is not a crime. People who have this disability should not be denied their freedom.

To accomplish anything worthwhile, we all must risk failure. People with disabilities must take risks, too — to test themselves, to grow.

Are mentally retarded adults like children?

No. They're treated like children sometimes by people who mean well but misunderstand. For instance, some people might encourage a woman with mental retardation who likes children to play with dolls. Instead, she could probably be trained to assist in a day-care center. A young man who spends his days playing with clay and coloring could be working in a greenhouse. Both these people could contribute to their community and to their own independence. Mentally retarded people need the good feelings that accomplishment brings. They need to grow up just like the rest of us.

What will mentally retarded children do when they grow up? Where will they live?

Most of them will get jobs. Some will work in places called sheltered workshops, where they will get special training and supervision. Many will work in regular jobs in the community. They may need special support and training at first. Sometimes the mentally retarded need more training than the new person at work.

Some people will continue living with their parents or, if they are severely disabled, in an institution. More and more, though, young adults with mental retardation move out on their own. Some live in group homes or in apartments with other retarded adults. Those with good living skills can live in apartments or houses on their own or with spouses or friends.

THINGS TO DO AND TALK ABOUT

Doing projects like the ones below will help you understand more about how people learn and about people who have mental retardation.

1. Are there children with mental retardation in your class? In your school? Ask your teacher if you can get to know one of these children by tutoring him or her when your own work is done.

2. Invite someone to speak to your class on the subject of rights for people with disabilities. Some local chapters of the organizations listed on page 46 might provide speakers. Ask your teacher to help you find someone to speak if your town has no local organizations.

3. Most of us learn better at some times than at others. We may learn things that matter to us more easily than we learn things we don't care about. Some of us learn better if we're relaxed. Some of us learn better when we're under pressure. Try a few of these experiments.

a) Have a friend write five phone numbers down on a piece of paper. Turn on the TV — loud! Now have a friend time you for three minutes while you try to memorize the numbers. When time is up, write down the numbers you remember. Have your friend pick five more phone numbers. Spend your three minutes of study time in a quiet place. Write down what you remember when your time is up. Did the setting affect what you remembered?

b) Give yourself five minutes to learn six lines from a poem. Tell your friend to dump ice water on your head if you can't remember the lines. Then give yourself another five minutes to learn six more lines. Reward yourself with a candy bar if you learn them. Does the idea of reward or punishment affect how well you learn?

c) Have a friend pick a topic from an encyclopedia.

Read for ten minutes and have your friend ask you ten questions about the material you read. Now pick a topic yourself, one that interests you but not one you know about already. Do the same experiment — ten minutes of reading, ten questions. Does your level of interest affect how much you remember from your reading?

Children with mental retardation, like most of us, learn best when rewarded. Praise is a great reward. So is the chance to use what they've learned. Most mentally retarded people will not learn as many things as a person with normal intelligence, but they may learn many things very well.

MORE INFORMATION ABOUT MENTAL RETARDATION — PLACES TO WRITE AND PEOPLE TO CALL

You can write to people at the organizations listed below for free material about mental retardation. Some of the organizations have state and local branches as well as the national offices listed here. Check your phone book and give them a call. Whether you call or write, give the reason for your interest so the people can send you the material that best suits your purpose.

Administration on Developmental Disabilities
Department of Health and Human Services
200 Independence Avenue SW
Washington, DC 20201

Association for Retarded Citizens
P.O. Box 6109
Arlington, TX 76006

Council for Exceptional Children
1920 Association Drive
Reston, VA 22091

Mainstream
1200 15th Street NW, Suite 403
Washington, DC 20005

National Down Syndrome Society
141 Fifth Avenue
New York, NY 10010

Special Olympics
1350 New York Avenue NW
Suite 500
Washington, DC 20005

MORE BOOKS ABOUT CHILDREN AND MENTAL RETARDATION

The books listed below are about people who are mentally retarded. They are about brothers, sisters, friends, even an uncle. They are also about understanding and accepting.

But I'm Ready to Go. Albert (Bradbury Press)
Find Debbie! Brown (Houghton Mifflin)
Just One Friend. Hall (Macmillan)
Kelly's Creek. Smith (Crowell Jr.)
*Like It Is: Facts and Feelings About Handicaps from Kids
    Who Know.* Adams (Walker)
A Look at Mental Retardation. Anders (Lerner)
Making Room for Uncle Joe. Litchfield (Whitman)
Martin Is Our Friend. Hasler (Abingdon)
Mental Retardation. Dunbar (Franklin Watts)
Me Too. Cleaver and Cleaver (Lippincott Jr.)
My Sister Is Different. Wright (Raintree)
Volunteer Spring. Long (Archway)

GLOSSARY OF WORDS ABOUT
MENTAL RETARDATION AND LEARNING

Understanding the words and phrases below will help you understand more about people with mental retardation and how we all learn.

abstract: an idea that is not based upon or easily verifiable through the five senses. Ideas about love, death, and loyalty are abstract.

concept: an idea or thought.

concrete: something that can be perceived through the senses (sight, hearing, touch, taste, or smell). A picture of a dog is concrete. The way a dog smells is concrete. So are the sound of its bark and the feel of its fur. So is the taste of a spoonful of vinegar.

developmental disability: a kind of disability that limits how much a person will learn and how fast he or she will develop. Mental retardation is a developmental disability.

early intervention: the practice of educating children from the time somebody notices their disability, if possible right after birth. The idea behind the practice is that valuable learning time is lost if therapies and programs for learning are delayed until a child would normally start school. Children who receive early intervention start school with more of the skills of other children their age.

expressive language: the kind of language we use to express our thoughts and feelings to others. (See *receptive language*.)

intelligence: one measure of our ability to learn and to think. Intelligence is measured by tests that may or may not give a full picture of our abilities.

intelligence quotient: also called IQ, the number a person is given after tests that measure the ability to learn. The average IQ is 100.

mainstreaming: teaching children with disabilities and nondisabled children together. Mainstreaming is sometimes called integration. It replaced the older system which put children with disabilities in classes and schools by themselves. All children today can learn more about themselves and others by sharing the same classroom.

mental retardation: a permanent condition that causes persons to learn more slowly than others and usually limits their level of understanding. A person who is mentally retarded will be slow to develop in all areas, both mental and physical.

motivation: something besides a task itself that inspires someone to do something. Praise and rewards for success are motivators. Punishment for failure is a motivator, too, but it is not as effective.

receptive language: the language that we understand when we hear someone else speaking or when we read. (See *expressive language*.)

INDEX

Franklin Pierce College Library

00039712